The Paw Paw Almanac & Reader

By
Steve Livingston Nagle
and
Jo Schaper

The Paw Paw Almanac
by Steve Livingston Nagle
and Jo Schaper

Paw Paw Poets Publishing
Pacific MO - Palm Desert CA

NOTES

• Sharp-eyed readers will note we are not consistent with the use of *Paw Paw, paw paw or pawpaw*. There is no universally accepted colloquial name for the *Asimina triloba* tree or fruit, so we are following the lead of General William Clark, who spelled "Sioux" 27 ways in his journals.Whatever gets the meaning across and the job done!

• Those same readers will note that though the book is all in the same font, sometimes that font size varies to accommodate line lengths. We are making the type as large as possible for our older readers. This is deliberate, and not an error. Thanks for understanding.

Table of Contents

What the Paw Paws Came to Know 1
We do not speak of anything important 2
Way Out Yonder 3
Rocking Horse 6
Confession of an Aeroplane Pirate 7
Return to Camp Zoe 9
Camp Zoe Lodge 13
The Legend of Buzzard Cave 14
I Remember Harry Fender.............................. 20
Phantom on the Mississippi 22
95th Meridian.. 26
Skylark Drive-In 27
Train Time... 29
Jenny Lee's Cabin 31
Pie in the Sky... 33
Fort Leonard Wood....................................... 34
PawPaw Sour Mash Brandy- Kenneth Thomas .. 38
Daphne on the Meramec............................... 40
Meramec River Song..................................... 43
Paw Paw Encyclopedia 45
Karkhagne in the Ozarks 46
Spieleologist 50
Land Below 52
River Des Peres Song.................................... 53

Table of Contents (continued)

The Hole in the Wall 55
Banjo Coyote... 59
Southwest Diner.. 61
The Great River State.................................... 62
Show Me The River Tonight............................ 63
Raccoon in the Ozarks.................................. 65
Missouri River Suite...................................... 66
Revelation at Big Muddy Refuge 72
Arrow Rock Banjo Song................................. 74
Oracle of Alley Spring 76
The Oracle Speaks Back 78
Alley Spring Water Breath............................. 80
Winter Gigging on the Current 81
Misty Waters.. 86
Airphoto Tufa Creek...................................... 87
The Tsalagi Syllabary 88
The Cherokee Farmer.................................... 89
A Pilgrimage to Trail of Tears State Park.......... 94
The Trail Where People Cried 98
Panorama 100
Composition in Black and Red 102
1522 on Kirkwood Hill................................ 104
Eclipses 105
The Day the Sun Went Away........................ 106

Table of Contents (continued)

Thelma and Doyle Johnston Tour America 108
The Returning 109
Down Bur Oak Road - Mary Litvan-Culler 111
Petroglyph 113
They Came Before Us - Jim Duncan 115
Mishebishu 119
Paw Paws Reprise 121
About Paw Paw Poets Publishing 122

Scattered through the Paw Paw Almanac & Reader you will find small advertisements for Missouri environmental non-profits (and a couple of businesses) who are deserving of support. These ads are our way of thanking them for the good they do to preserve and protect our cultural and natural resources while helping people learn about them, and become active stewards themselves.

Author's Preface

One can say an orange is citrus. Or an apple is crisp or tart. There is a school of thought that different taste buds pick up on different aspects of a pawpaw: the rich messy pulp offers different flavors and remembrances of other fruit depending on one's experience.

Such is the case with The Paw Paw Almanac & Reader. What you find in it depends partly on what you bring to it.

The two of us bring very different life experiences to this book, but we both see stories and poems all around us. A common love of the outdoors and American folk history runs through here— the mixture that some call Americana. We share a love of "the road less traveled—" of an individual approach to living and making expressive sense of what we have seen. Sometimes traditionally expressed, and sometimes not.

We love to tell stories. These are Midwestern stories. We have a book of Western stories in the works. Our aim is to communicate with an easy readable style and a hold in your hand format not requiring any devices.

Come along with us on this Paw Paw adventure. And see what it tastes like to you.

What the Paw Paws Came to Know

Two pawpaw trees
Swaying in the breeze
Down in the bottoms of the Meramec
Each had believed
They came from seeds
planted by a crow who had the knack
To talk raccoon
In the light of the moon
They grew to have each other's back
Under green umbrellas side by side.

Then one day
a naturalist came
held a class beneath their branches
Gave a lecture
Without conjecture
about propagation of pawpaw patches
They learned the truth
Down to their roots
About their sideways circumstances,
In the aromatic organic soil:
Not lovers but rhizome twins

twining together beneath green earth
Living separate, but always together
Two pawpaw trees swaying in the breeze
Secret sap siblings of a common birth.
J.S.

"We do not speak of anything important--
only poetry."

To grasp at essences while stuck in daily muck,
Of crisis followed by task by crisis,
To draw one's breath from surface living,
Embrace the touch, the ability to feel the pulse
of the universe beyond the busy-ness,
this is the real job we do— erase the harshness
that denies us touch when it rises unasked
To see beyond that veil, to take the chance beyond lust
To become so vulnerable to passing cosmic winds
the sleigh ride of saints throughout the universe
To try to write that wind, focused upon the message
of two spirits soaring, the waterfall of flame and fire
tumbling our husks into angels, growing wings together.
J.S.

Painting by Gary R. Lucy

Way Out Yonder

One midsummer day
I asked my farm cousin
"Where is over yonder
Is it far away?"

"Not too far, just past
The outhouse down by the fence
Maybe to the pond but not beyond."

"Then how far is way out yonder
Is it a place we could go?'
This caused him to pause and ponder.
"It's a place way out yonder

In the wide open spaces
Where the prickly pear and purple sage grow."

"How do we get there?"
I wanted to know
"And what will we see?"
"Tall mountains and yellow valleys
Where wild horses and burros run free –
The hills where rivers rushing
Tumble down to the sea."
"And what can we do
When we get way out there?"
'We can watch the antelope leap in the air
We can follow the buffalo 'cross the prairie so fair
And pick wildflowers for grandmother's hair."

"Maybe tomorrow we can find our way there
To way out yonder if we double dog dare.
Is there a map to show us the way
Can we get back by the end of the day?"

"We can map our own trail
Starting just over yonder

Where the fox and the quail
And rabbits meander ..."
"We'll cross the muddy old creek
Through the pasture and timber
Then turn somewhere west past December...
By April or May we'll be half way there
The journey will take more than a day
To way out yonder
Where the prairie dogs play.

"While the old bird dog is snoring
Before our chores in the morning
We could leave without warning..."
"That would make Mama cry."
Down by the barn just over yonder

We came to decide
Before the rooster had crowed
And the cow was milked dry
We would wait 'til we're older
For way out yonder
Then give it a try.
S.L.N.

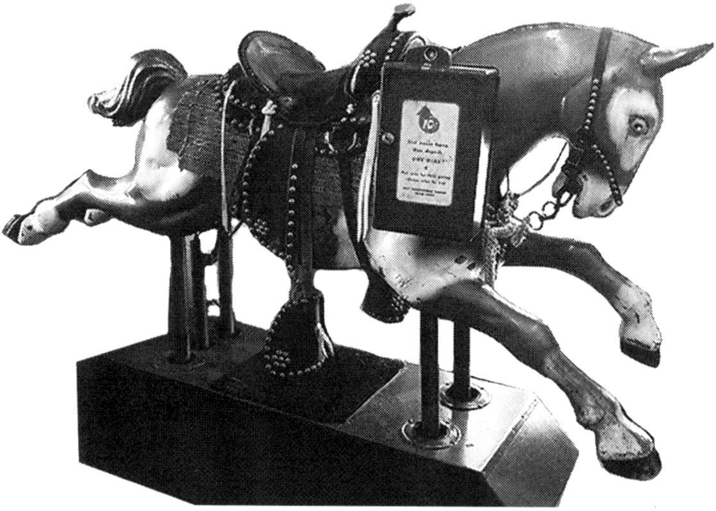

Rocking Horse

The rocking horse is out of order
Put out to pasture so they say—
The hardware store pinto saddled and bridled
All the young children galloped away.
Hard to figure why it still stands there
The coin box weathered by too many quarters
A two minute ride, from Ozarks to sagebrush
Abandoned by our grandsons and daughters—
"Where is the screen? There's nothing to see."
They look at us quizzically when we say
Mounted on that horse we could ride forever
Cowboys and Indians to the close of day.
J.S.

Confession of an Aeroplane Pirate

Not a pilot but a pirate was I
When I stole an aeroplane and
took to the sky

A flight of fancy
I knew it was chancy
To pull such a stunt
For a short little runt
With a burning yearning to fly

A teenage daredevil
of ill repute
Life without a parachute

We tugged the old Jenny
Out of the barn
My cousin stood nervously by
Bidding me not to try
But for me it was do or die
I climbed in the cockpit
Spied the ignition and stick
The old engine coughed and
Rumbled alive
Down the field she rolled
And the throttle took hold and soon
we were lifted on high.

Over the field I flew like a turkey
All ruffled and noisy and looking to land
But what was ahead I thought I was dead
the trees were too close at hand

Pulling back on the stick
We lifted so quick
The old Jenny flew like a bird
I kicked the rudder bar and banked around
And the farmer stood down on the ground

How we landed I can't recall
That aeroplane had plowed his field
He shook his fist and cussed me out
So bad was I without a doubt
But to regret I would not yield

Into the woods we ran
To Granny's house not far away
Me and my cousin in secret bond
Not known until this day.
S.L.N.

RETURN TO CAMP ZOE

The names of horses and riders
Carved into the wood inside the barn
Where she stood touching with her fingers
The summers of her youth
Maybe not so long ago
This place she remembers
That carved a record in her soul
This place this hiding place
In the Ozark hills
Where the laughing waters flow
This place called old Camp Zoe.

What remains is the barn
Down in the holler
And crowning the grassy hill
The old stone lodge still there
Wanting restoration standing in
A state of disrepair needing
Someone to care
Quietly softly she enters and
Steps upon the old plank floor
She could hear the children laughing
Talking just like it was before.

She could hear the loudspeaker wake up call
That echoed off the rocky wall
From the bluffs above the creek
Reveille to start the day
Taps trumpeted a lullaby to sleep
the promise of tomorrow
And her soul and her friends to keep.
The mess hall call
was the happy sound for all
"Soupy – Soupy – Soupy
Come get your soup, Come get your flubber--"

Karo syrup and peanut butter.

Shooting the bow and arrow
Weaving lanyards, swimming in Sinkin' Creek
Running through the woods playing hide n seek
Horseback trail rides and campfire songs
Those summer days seemed endless so enchanting
And so long - like a never ending song
From morning light to the man in the moon
Then suddenly summer was gone too soon.

She remembered watching meteor showers
And shooting stars, campfire stories like the one
That Winkie told about the Indian maiden and
The enemy brave she loved so dear their
Star-crossed love they couldn't hide nor
Live in shadows or in fear
So together they did leap
Into a deep blue Round Spring
Like a deep blue wishing well
Where now their spirits forever dwell.

Along the native stone pathways

And these woodland trails
Where children use to play
She hears the wild birds singing
And the promise of Nature's way.
She returns with old camp friends
To paddle
Down that laughing crystal stream
Together again
to re-live that Camp Zoe summer dream.
S.L.N.

"Behold the rain which descends from heaven upon our vineyards; there it enters the roots of the vines, to be changed into wine; a constant proof that God loves us, and loves to see us happy."

Zoe Lodge

The stones are quilt tilted
Laid end on side, sandstone and
limestone mixed on concrete.
The children must have helped—

no flatness, jumblestone set
chunks of chert and ironstone—
Built with what they were given
a fieldstone delight, crystallized chunks

of blue sky and pines and skipping stones
A place to gather along the creek
ironweed and spring water and fish
red clay beneath the dark sky stars.
J.S.

The Legend of Buzzard Cave

For Frank Dunbar 1899-1983

Deep in the woods of the Ozark hills
A few farmsteads still linger on
Nailed together in rustic charm
Writing stories on the wind
From every field and farm.

Grandfather told me of the Osage
Who claimed the land their own
The Sac and Fox and Cherokee
Trails west to unknown homes.

The creeks and rivers and secret hollows
Wrote their stories upon the land
Old warriors and their faded glory
Then Grandfather said to me:

"Their souls are watching still
Hiding behind every tree
Watching all the sacred places to
Keep them wild and free.'

He told me of a cave he found
A hideout from long ago
I followed him everywhere
That I was old enough to go.

He spoke often of Buzzard Cave
An adventure quest he stirred in me
Then one day he took me there
That place called Buzzard Cave

Down the haunted hollow
We hiked, Grandfather
My cousin and me
Tree shadows glooming over us
Cedar, oak and hickory--

Into the valleys of dogwood,
Redbud, sassafras and pawpaw
Yonder in a farmers field
We heard the plaintive song
Of a day-disturbed whippoorwill
An awakening remembered still

As we drew deeper into the woods
Ferns and moss flourished, limestone grew slick
Leaves and rocks underfoot where short legs slipped
Ledge water dripped from underground springs.

My cousin asked, "Will we see
The Grim Reaper and other scary things?"
"Not today," Grandfather said,
As he pointed to a copperhead
Slithering away.

A red headed woodpecker
Flickered to a dead tree
"Are we getting closer
To the cave?" I asked, "Are we?"

Grandfather said, "I think
Our quest will soon reach an end;
If I remember, it's just around this bend."
Our imaginations went wild
The mystery of Buzzard Cave
Would soon be solved —
The old family story
The legend and the glory
On this day resolved.

As we got closer and closer
Quietly we wondered
What would we find?

A wolf or bear sleeping there?

Lots of stones and ancient bones?
Shaman pictures painted on the wall?
Pirate swords and rusty guns
A den of snakes? Silver and gold?
Jesse James hideout? Treasures of old?
Grandfather looked and looked again
He pointed up under the rocky ledge.

"Holy Smoke?" he exclaimed as if he
Was surprised he found it. "There it is!"
We'd already scampered beneath the trees
Up the muddy side of the steep hollow.
Turned around just to make sure
Grandfather would follow.

A tanglewood of saplings and vine
Guarded the opening of the cave
The machine gun staccato of the woodpecker
Led us upward, and beyond —
Then there we stood peering into darkness
Where was the flashlight? Back at the farm
On the workbench inside the barn!

Coming from somewhere
Deep inside the ground
The sound of water dripping, dripping
Sculpting limestone into a cathedral
Then by some strange timing
The dipping sun shone into this tomb
Into the mystical mysterious gloom.

Oh, what we saw on that day

We promised never to say
We vowed never to tell —
My dear cousin and I all these years
Have kept our secret so well.
Grandfather was my flint knapper
He sharpened my imagination
Polished my dull knife on whetstone;
He was the hickory bow, I was the arrow
He was the tree I was the sparrow
And never more than that Ozark day
I learned to explore more than a cave

This is what he gave to me
On all the paths we shared:
The way to walk with enchantment
And though silver and gold are the common
measure
He taught imagination is the buried treasure
And I know he's always there.
S.L.N.

I Remember Harry Fender

I still remember Harry Fender
Driving that boat down the Mississloppy.

My brother, of course, waited
For the Three Stooges movies to appear
On our big black and white TV.
After school, something to do
To stay invisible, lest Mom press us
Into peeling carrots or diaper service
Before it was time for supper.
"Captain 11" he was called, but we knew better,
Knew he really was Sam Clemens somehow
Preserved, commanding the pilothouse, with cigar
One hundred years ongoing. Knew beyond the rail
The real Mississippi flowed, in living color &
The rows of onscreen children cheering were
Imaginary pasteboard cutouts in grayscale,
While Mr. Fender, resplendent in blue uniform
And gold braid, kept his footing when waves
rocked the deck
As he steered between stone piers of Eads's Bridge.

While the television played at Grandma's
We heard the towboats blaring eight blocks over
The intricate filgereed calliope —called cally-ope
Of the SS Admiral passing the brewery,
South beneath the last remaining mound,
Past the clang of the shipyard meeting metal
At the foot of Iron Street. Brother adored the mayhem
While I marveled at the white curls and moustache
Wondered by what hoodoo the wraith of Twain
Both steered and spoke the language of the river,
I knew the television show was just a disguise
A put-on for adults who could not accept the truth:
At night, it was the studio that went away,
And the moon shown down on the Mississloppy
Banjos playing as the showboat passed.
Yes, I remember Harry Fender.
J.S.

PHANTOM ON THE MISSISSIPPI

(REQUIEM FOR THE WHITE CLOUD)

A heavy fogbank clung to the River
As I boarded the Pathfinder
On an early morning in August
Casting off from the mooring
Smoothly churning, motor moaning,
The propellers turning.

Beginning our journey south
From the port of Hannibal
The River was smooth as a lake
I was mesmerized
By the Pathfinder's wake
But the fog was still dense
and did not break.

I stepped forward to
The front of the tow
Hearing the sound
Of a steamboat whistle
Off the starboard bow
Out from the mist and
Slow rise of the fog I saw
What appeared to be a white apparition
Taking shape, a faint image of
An old Mississippi River paddle steamer
Slowly traveling up river.

It had not passed us yet
Coming through the fog
I could see its bow and
Filigreed decks.

As it chugged closer
I saw the wheelhouse with no pilot
Nor a soul on board – Oh, my Lord
My Lord! What strange phantom is this?
A riverboat ghost sailing out of the mist.
As this great phantom steamer

Floated on by I heard a bell toll
And an invisible man cry:
"Oh White Cloud you beautiful
Steam boat, you weren't suppose to burn
You weren't suppose to die
Now we've all gone to that
Sweet bye and bye."

We continued our course
On the Pathfinder tow
Gliding down the Mississippi
Ahead of the flow – smoothly
Navigating the main channel
"We're goin down to Cairo good bye, good bye –
The fog bank had risen,
The River ran high
"We're goin down to
Cairo, good bye Liza Jane."
I looked astern and the ghostly riverboat
Had disappeared without a trace
All day I kept hearing a choir singing
By the grace of the river
From a faraway place.

And generous is the river giving us
secrets and lore:
"In the sweet bye and bye
We shall meet on that beautiful shore
And our spirits shall sorrow no more
And our spirits shall sorrow no more."

As this great phantom steamer
Floated on by I heard a bell toll
And an invisible man cry
"Oh White Cloud, you beautiful steamboat
You weren't supposed to die.
Now we've all gone to that
Sweet bye and bye."
S.L.N.

This poem was inspired by real events. I took a photo of the old style riverboat that appeared on the river that day coming through the fog like a ghost. On May 17, 1849, the White Cloud steam boat moored on the St. Louis waterfront caught fire which ended up destroying 23 other riverboats and 430 buildings in the city. It was the worst disaster in St. Louis history. During the Civil War many riverboats also met their demise. Then in 1865 1,169 passenger, mostly veterans anxious to go home, met their deaths when the boilers exploded on board the Sultana. There were glory days and tragic days in the great riverboat era. This poem is dedicated to those riverboats and dauntless travelers.-S.L.N.

95th Meridian

The wind from the west comes in forever
Bumps up against the ridge dropped loess
Sweeps the plains east on a grassy promise
A shirr in the ears, the audible evening dust.
The hat and the squint and the rolling walk

(Men on high boot heels trying desperately
To stay macho) and I can pick them out by ear:
The rustle in the nose, gravel in the throat, from
I swear, too many hours in dark and cold theaters
Watching horse opera. They have a swagger

Most people have long forgot—a way to stay in charge
A birthright of casting words into the teeth of the breeze
Which never stops. No one talks for long. Silence
Can last for days. When words resume, that nasal tenor
Tunes to storytelling, and you'd better be prepared:

Life upon the 95th meridian, where the wind and sky
Broadcast the weather, where men still favor leather,
Where tall grass waves on forever and these men
Easily slip one hundred years to the frontier still carried
Like an invisible tin star, upon their city clothes.

J.S.

Skylark Drive-In

Memories take me back
To Dad's '53 Pontiac
At the Skylark Drive-In movie
Pretending I was Audie Murphy.
Mom made the popcorn
Dad fell asleep.

And I watched a double feature
From the big back seat
I could see clearly then
Just like being there
To a place called the Code of the West
Beyond the hundredth meridian
Where right was right
And wrong was wrong
And men were put to the test.

Then I grew older and had a date
at the Skylark Drive-In
we stayed out late
By the time I took her home
The whole world had changed
Nothing was the same
The Code of the West was rearranged
It was twilight at the Skylark:

Younger eyes gazed at video games
The Frog Hop Ballroom became bowling lanes
The light burned out at the Skylark
There we were, alone in the dark...

Where have all the heroes gone?
Will they return in the new light of dawn?
I cried, calling "Come back Shane..."
"Shane come back!"
"We need you, mother needs you."
I cried out again as he rode his horse
to the far Tetons and out of sight.
"Shane come back ...come back Shane."

Take me back to the Skylark
Take me back one more time
Take me back to the Drive-In movie
Alan Ladd was a friend of mine.

S.L.N.

Train Time

There's a light at the end of the tunnel
The brakeman's waving at us
Ready to switch at Yeatman Wye
A turning with little fuss.

He's ten again, gone to the station
With Grandpa to pick up the mail,
And Uncle Todd's waiting at the M&I Bridge
For George to come ride the rails.

The Mark Twain Zephyr's stopped for him,
The troop train waiting once more
Pistons hissing, impatiently insisting
To take the young soldier to war.

His next long ride, home again, to a bride
Durango to Silverton with Rose—
The train round the tree and then there were three,
Next, a son, and some more, so it goes.

From the high cab of 4960 he sees
Doc Roberts' trainyard turned to a park
The age of steam shrunk to WF&P
The place he fnally gets to play his part.

Now the train's left the station for the last time,
Pressures all high, full steam ahead,
Casey at the throttle, Steve Broady a firin'
And walking the boxcar roofs--Red.
J.S.

JENNY LEE'S CABIN

Deep down in Dallas County in a place called "Four Mile," at a distance of four miles from Longlane, Missouri, there set a cabin that breathed cold air and snow in the winter and the fragrance of wildflowers and hay in the summer.

Great-Grandma Jenny Lee, part Cherokee, lived there with her purple violets on the windowsill and wild apple pies baking in her cast iron oven.

My visits there as a boy child were life-changing even then. She made for me a patchwork quilt which I still have and use. She covered me with it. And when I settled down in the iron-framed feather bed, then she sat in front of a mirror in the room and brushed her long silvery hair. Her eyes were dark and smiling and she had an easy laugh. Her face, with the crowsfeet smile, was always tan and her hair put up in a bun each day. In the morning fresh eggs were gathered, biscuits cooked and hot gravy from flour, milk and lard, and hot oatmeal with fresh cream were on the wooden table. I learned the word "pioneer" and believed that was the life for me in Jenny Lee's cabin.

There were old Indian trails out there and what must have been a remnant prairie or perhaps it was a sheltered glade and a spring-fed pond, where she took me by the hand and led me through the prairie grass and showed me the herbs and wildflowers that lined the path. Then down at the spring, we harvested watercress, which she mixed in Jell-O with slivers of carrots from her garden. She always stopped to listen to the song birds or to watch a hawk in the sky and showed me the shapes of leaves on the trees.

As I grew, the wonder and enchantment of nature and discovery were grafted to my soul, and this is where it began— at Jenny Lee's Cabin, with the pioneering memories of my Great-Grandma Jenny Lee Livingston-Hill.

Grandma Jenny Lee was a writer. She wrote letters— good letters, always with a pencil, informative letters. I saw her many times but never enough in my growing up years, Still folded up in a Bible she gave me in first grade I keep one of those letters. In that letter she wrote *"...I came home and it snowed, the beautiful kind with big flakes that looked like flowers falling and playing tag."*

It was the last letter she wrote to me— when I was in the Army— postmarked February, 1967.
S.L.N.

PIE IN THE SKY

Wild apple, rhubarb or gooseberry pie
Great Granny's heavenly pies in the sky
Golden brown crust is a crust you can trust
If heaven will take me to that place way up high
Then happily I die for her pie in the sky.

Oh wild gooseberries baked in a pie or spread on a cake
Eat em in the cabin or a picnic by the lake...
Those wild berries with the tart sour taste
I can eat them anywhere leavin' notta one to waste.
S.L.N.

FORT LEONARD WOOD

We were the Fighting Blue Devils
Of Fort Lost in the Woods
In our prime at a time
Our intentions were good
We marched to the beat
Of a cadence drum,
Knowing later that year
We would meet again
In Viet Nam
Where some of us
Would stay forever young —

Courage we mustered to
Be unafraid
Such was the lesson
Of our Training Brigade.

The drill sergeant yelled:
“Are there any drummers out there?”
I raised my hand   I was so unaware

With my rifle on my back
            And the drum on my leg
I beat the rhythm for marching

No matter the pace.

Prum prum … prum-prum prum
Day in day out I beat on the drum

And a hundred men sang
" I wanna be an airborne ranger
  I wanna live a life of danger
  Prum prum per ruppa prum prum."

We crawled on our bellies under barbed wire
Over sharp rocks under
Machine gun fire—

Then we marched again.

“Around the tree
She tied a yellow ribbon,
She tied it for her soldier
who was far far away--
Far away — far away
She tied it for her soldier
who was far-far away....”

Prum prum...prum, prum - prum.

In the hut of gas
we took off our masks
The drill sergeant shouted “No retreat!
Don’t ever ask...”
Back in formation again
We did ”Dress right, DRESS”
Column left— March!”

“Hup - two three four
What are we fighting for?”
“Hey Bo Diddley have you heard
We’re gonna jump from a big iron bird
Hey Bo Diddley Hey Bo Diddley...”

We were the Fighting Blue Devils
Of Fort Lost in the Woods
In our prime at a time when intentions were good
We marched to the beat of a cadence drum
Our boots pounded in unison
Hup – two-three – four
I still hear the cannons roar
Prum, prum, prum-prum-prum

We marched to the beat
of a cadence drum
We're on our way to Viet Nam
Where some of us
Would stay forever young —
S.L.N.

PawPaw Sour Mash Brandy

Kenneth V. Thomas III

Ingredients:

50 lbs. fresh pawpaws

35 lbs. sugar

10 oz. Champagne yeast

40 gallons potable water

2 -55 gallon non-leaky barrels or a huge iron cauldron

A canoe paddle. Wash the paddle with soap and hot water.

Skin and seed the pawpaw fruit.

Put all ingredients in a clean 55 gallon barrel and mix thoroughly with the paddle.

Heat the water to 85^0 F. Toss in the yeast, and stir to mix.

Let it ferment for 5-7 days or until the bubbling stops.

Once it's done fermenting, you rack it off by siphoning off the clear liquid into the pot and fire it up. You don't want any sediment to enter the pot. It may scorch and ruin the flavor. With the proof of the liquor being 140+ you want to carry as much flavor of the pawpaw over. See when you distill, a lot of the flavor is lost. That's why I put soooooo much pawpaw in the mash. I hope it makes sense.

MERAMEC RIVER RECREATION ASSN.

"LET THE RIVER FLOW"

Lower Meramec River Watershed

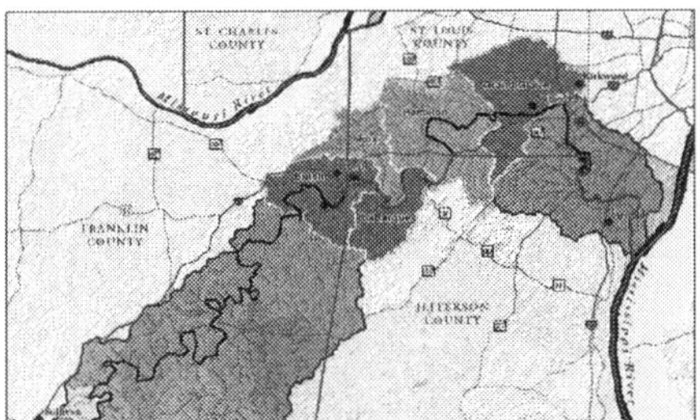

Map from EWGCOG Planning

https://www.facebook.com/MeramecRRA/

Daphne on the Meramec

Young lady sprung from a nymph and the river,
Sister to springs to water falls to flowing streams
Invisible among bluebells ringing in the breeze
Golden flowers shone then like the sun in her eyes
She hides in the bottomlands, in shades and sighs.

Virginal, her beauty blinds mere mortals. She's a wisp
They only think they have seen and then dismiss
She hides in plain sight, her bow and arrow unseen
Lives on sprouts and the nuts of trees, a harvested rabbit
And the stunned dead squirrel fallen at her feet.

She thought nothing of the morning that she found
The thinnest galena arrow impaled in her shoulder.
It barely hurt. She pulled it out and let it bleed.
It healed quickly, but left a scar, a cloud on her heart
A veil on her soul, a sudden fear of being seen.

When the red-bearded blond adventurer appeared,
He laughed too loudly, tore down branches in his haste.
He scattered light everywhere. No place to hide. She took flight,
Flew like the wind through dark spaces, but he pursued,
though fleet of foot, she waned, unable to keep pace.

She called the river. “Father, sacred lifeblood, save me,
Rise up in flood, separate me from that brightness!”
Nothing happened. The river glinted, tumbled along
Her cries muffled in its song. “Oh grandmother Gaia
Hide me in a fog!” The light burned brighter and the heat

Grew too intense. “You will be mine!” shrieked the stranger,
“As I cause the plants to grow, you will yield. You will yield!”
No! I shall never!” Clouds rolled overhead, and the river rose
Mired her feet in the bottomlands. As her hair tangled into trees
Her slender arms hardened; fingers fanned into large green leaves
And her soft breasts turned into pawpaw fruit.
J.S.

Meramec River Basin

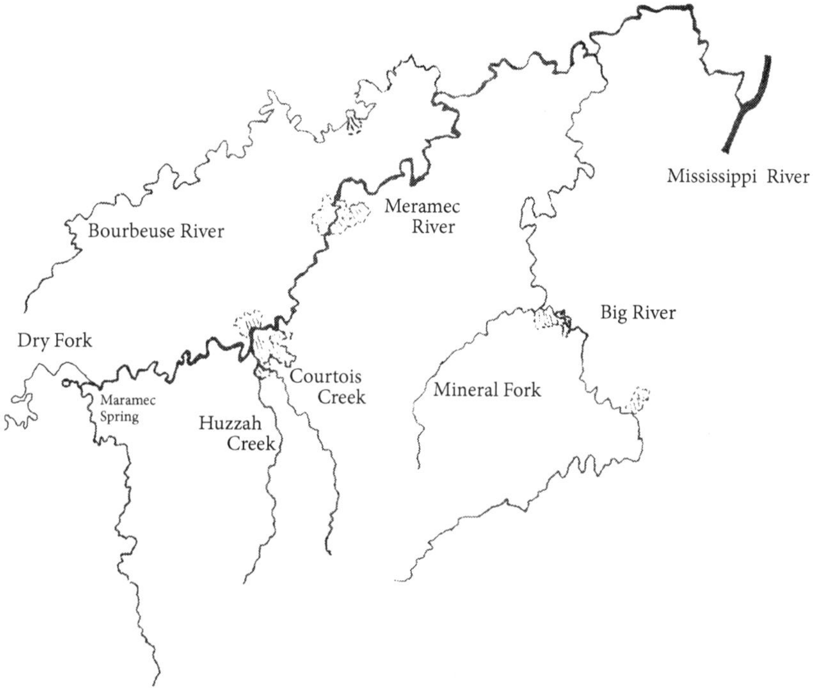

MERAMEC RIVER SONG

From the fountains of the Ozarks to the Mississippi shore
Ol' Meramec River runs free forever more
From the Ozark Mountains to the Mississippi shore
The people of the River live in legend and in lore
Let the River flow, let it flow
Hallelujah let the River flow

The River has many voices
some are weak some are strong
If you listen with your heart
You will hear the river song
Hallelujah let the River flow...

Have you found the pearly mussels
Along the gravel bars
Or spied a rusty levee
That once was trucks and cars
Have you paddled your canoe
in the sun and rain or snow
or gazed upon the River
in the Valley far below
Hallelujah! Let the River flow

Does your spirit take wing at the first sign of Spring
Do you feel redeemed when the little Bluebird sings
Or see a Great Blue Heron sailing 'cross the trees
Or touched a Hellbender and felt the Summer breeze
Have you tugged out a tire
Covered in river mud
And mounted it on your bow
Paddling down the River
With Viking plunder on your prow

Hallelujah let it flow
Hallelujah let the River flow
The River rocks and the River rolls
The River sings and the River flows
The River gives and the River knows
The River lives, let it move your Soul
Hallelujah Hallelujah Let the River flow!

S.L.N.

The Meramec River Song

https://www.youtube.com/watch?v=593j1iU7Nvc

ᏝᏄᎩ  ᏝᏄᎩ

The Story of the Paw Paw

The Paw Paw tree grows in the Southern and Midwestern United States, along creeks and rivers, in the riparian corridor. It is a graceful understory tree with large, often five-fingered leaves. The tree is semi-tropical, growing best in damp environments and most well known for its fruit, which ripens in September. The gree three to five inch long ovals contain large brown seeds. The pulp is undescribable--sweet,with a custard texture and a flavor similar to citrus, cherry and melon mixed together.

Paw Paw bark was twisted by Southeastern U.S. Natives into cord and rope. The seeds are inedible, but have been ground to a powder to discourage lice. Other folk uses for pawpaw were to fight fevers or vomiting, but there is no evidence they actually work. The fruit are usually eaten raw, but can be dried with other fruit to make a sort of pemmican. DeSoto first described pawpaws to Europeans. People have to be fast to get the fruit before raccoons, squirrels, possums and deer do, but sufficiently advanced green fruit will ripen if kept in a refrigerator a couple of days. The fruit can be fermented into a sort of cloudy sweetish beer. A paw paw patch is often a single plant joined by the roots. J.S.

Ozark creature possible explanation for Missouri karst

One explanation for Missouri's karst landscape lies at the confluence of the woodsman's craft and the caver's fascination with the hollow underground.

Speleogeneticists have pondered the origins of Missouri springs and caves for just over a century, coming up with a complex story of soluble rock, adequate rainfall, a tilted, cracked and faulted stratigraphy, and an epic story requiring a billion years of geological history to accomplish.

The truth may be shorter. Much shorter – about the height and length of a dachshund. The story originates at the flagship university, the University of Missouri – Columbia, so it must be true.

There are no photos of this beast – the Ozark karkhagne. According to one artist's rendition, this little seen Ozark beast has the head of a dragon, the body of a turtle, the legs of a lion, and a forked tail, which looks like an adder's tongue. A game camera, baited with sassafras sawdust and diesel fuel near the West Fork of the Gasconade River for the last five years, has returned no pictures so far.

Karkhagnes are known to chew through carbonate rocks, having a special fondness

for local dolomites and limestones set as survey markers at section corners, according to one of the few written sources – that of Ed Woods, from the 1964 *Missouri Log*, the MU forestry club yearbook of yore.

"I knew Ed Woods," said Dr. Dave Larsen, Forestry Department chair at MU. "He was one of the first Pioneer Forest foresters. The students back then asked him to write down the story for them. I think he made it up in the early 50s."

The editor of that long ago publication, not Mr. Woods, claimed that the only way a karkhagne could be seen was through the bottom of an "Old Forester" bottle, and claimed that Woods was at the time one of the few living experts on the karkhagne.

Though Woods' article says that karkhagne traveled backwards, brushing out tracks with its bristly whiskers, it seems more likely that foresters never encounter them because they live much of their lives underground. With a diet of chalky rock, it is fairly obvious that the karks need to drink frequently. Our beautiful speleothems may indeed be a result of an unmentionable bodily process of the creatures. One species' dung may be another's treasure.

I first encountered the karkaghne (note spelling change) on a family vacation shortly after Wood's article appeared. While camped in the Clark National Forest, we took the 30-mile drive along Forest Road 2233, designated as the Karkaghne Trail (or officially, the Karkaghne Scenic Drive). The drive (more or less) reached west to east from the Marcoot fire tower to our campsite.

Before the Buick Mine, (which now sits near where the route crosses Hwy. KK) you could drive the length of the Karkaghne Trail and not see anything but trees, gravel road, and occasional views of the Ozark Mountains.

No doubt the native karkaghne were deeply disturbed by this intrusion of their territory. When the mine moved in, and forest growth obscured the vistas, the Scenic Drive lost its popularity as a tourist attraction.

Perhaps the creatures were aghast at the 15-ton per scoop loaders that could hollow out the land far faster than even a squadron of little karks. Perhaps too many St. Louis tourists were lost to karkaghne mothers, prowling for food for their offspring, traditionally born 40 miles from air, land or water. According to Woods' article, the karkhagne loses no encounters and consumes all the evidence, so it's unlikely we'll ever know.

Not much is known about the kark's life history. Dr. Carla Cagston, noted karknologist, believes they hatch from cylindrical aluminum eggs, similar in shape and size to beer cans. "The mothers lay these eggs in nest-like structures," she said. "That's why the carbonate geologists call these areas karst."

Evasive as cavefish, and less sociable than hodags, karkaghnes have evolved to use the absence of light to see, and therefore have never lost their eyesight, with the development of orbs to augment rods and cones in their eye structure. Cavers are encouraged to wear high-topped rubber footwear, as these reticent beings love to bite, and then unravel the waxed thread of most sewn leather boots. When this happens the unwary caver tends to lose his or her sole in the Ozarks and is doomed to return time and time again.

Twenty years after that camping trip, the karkaghne surfaced again. Two sections of the Ozark Trail, from Oates to Sutton's Bluff, and thence to Blair Creek are now named for this "mythical creature in forest folklore."

According to Larsen, The Missouri Society of American Foresters paid tribute to the karkaghnae (another spelling change) by naming its highest professional service award for the kark. “The award is a little wooden sculpture of the karkaghnae,” he said. “And there is the Karkaghnae Club. This is an organization of people whose purpose is the betterment of Missouri’s forests. The original idea was to provide a forum where members could express opinions concerning forestry without fear of retribution.

No one has ever lived to tell if karkaghnes make any noise, so if you every travel underground, be alert and aware, and carry a roll of Tums with you. Legend say they can temporarily be distracted with that sweet treat, just as bells provide a quick bear getaway. If it is nothing that you hear, and nothing that you see as the walls crumble and brick orange clay surges toward you, run for the entrance before you fall victim to a pack of Ozark karkhagnes.

J.S.

Spieleologist

Step right up, step in here
see this formation, the Elephant’s Ear,
only eight bucks, folks,
for an hour of cool. We’ve got
walkways, stairways, rampways
and always good Ozark entertainment.

Your guide has been trained
scientifically, knows all them facts
of caveology. Yeah, folks, it's twice
as dark in a cave at night
we know it cause we measured it
with an eighteen inch yardstick.

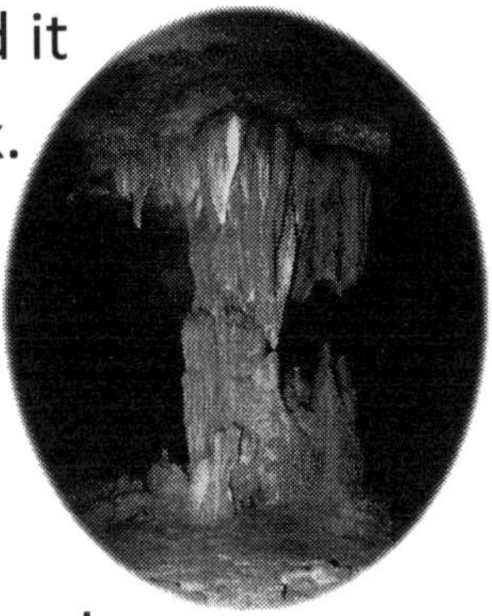

Directly below this point
lies the center of the earth.
That formation there contains
a million dollar's worth
of rare travertine cave onyx. Here's
the Madonna formation, and there's her son.
We have something to please everyone.

Watch your head please,
watch your step. The exotic
cave plants are to your right,
Jesse's treasure to your left.
We've got nine miles
of undiscovered passage here
but we haven't found it yet.
Guano Mountain's just ahead.
Watch where you step.

J.S.

Land Below

Where she has been the sky has never seen
heaven underground, light studded ceiling stars
and bats– not eagles– guarding
a mud slogged stoop and crawl.
Amid the stones she's always alone
her eyes seeking tiny wonders--
helictites between broken soda straws
cave coral around the base
of chopped down stalagmites.
This quiet holds her secret delight--
just breath and water dripping.

It's been her vision always, since
her red clay and crystal days--
mute before the blue upwellings.
If it were up to her, perhaps,
she'd stay below forever
grow pallid as her fish.
Knowing the impossibility of this
she smiles a mud-smeared smile--
light blinding the crickets as she bellies out
through dirt and leaves and rock.
J.S.

The River des Peres

(Life in the River – Banjo Key of G)

The River des Peres is an urban stream 9.3 miles long from the headwater creeks north of the city to its confluence with the Mississippi River. As with many urban waterways, it has been maligned and mistreated. For purposes of sanitation and flood control, the river section that flowed through Forest Park was buried in large tunnels before the St. Louis World's Fair. The recent Park master plan mimics the river's historic riparian system with flowing waters, wetlands, savannas and prairie.

There's life in the river
There's life in the river
There's life in the River des Peres
(repeat)

There's fish in the water, birds in the air
There's fish in the water, birds in the air
There's fish in the water, birds in the air
There's life in the River Des Peres

We have a dream about
A backyard urban stream
No more sewers running there
Many people really care
Never give up in despair
Clean water for the children everywhere

It's not easy being green
So come and join the bold Stream Team
Take action, don't just dream
Come join the bold Stream Team
Clean water for the children everywhere.
There's life in the River des Peres!!!
There's life in the River des Peres...
S.L.N.

THE HOLE IN THE WALL

The painted billboard with the big finger pointed to the old dilapidated house.

The sign beckoned in big letters:

"SEE THE HOLE IN THE WALL

From

The Bullet That Killed Jesse James"

"Stop here to see Jesse James' Home."

That's the way I remember it. Right there off the main road we called the Belt Highway – State Highway 169, in my hometown of St. Joe, Missouri.

As a boy, we learned early on about Jesse James and the Pony Express and Cherry Mash Rounders. Oh and don't forget the Stetson Hat factory and Western Tablet where the red covered Big Chief Tablets were made and the old Goetz Brewery where my Dad managed the brewing and bottling of old fashioned American lager. Yes sir, we had a lot to be proud of in that little river town.

The wood frame old home of Jesse James had been moved out to a "busier" more commercially strategic location and over the years from lack of paint the wood sides had turned to smoky black.

One day I finally got my parents to buy a ticket to see inside. I had to see the bullet hole. Well there we were standing, staring at the hole which was a big as the wall itself or what was left of the wall. Souvenir hunters had been carving away at the bullet hole for years to take out little pieces and big pieces of lath, plaster and wood that surrounded the actual bullet hole. I imagine scattered around the country lost in drawers and keep sake boxes are the relics carved out of the hole in the wall - saved for no religious purpose but maybe over the years reminded the keepers of their own mortality.

There wasn't much else to see that I remember. But I did think of poor Jesse and learned never to straighten a picture hanging crooked on the wall with your back turned to somebody you don't trust.

The old Greek Revival style one story dwelling was originally located at 1218 Lafayette Street in St. Joseph and moved out to the Belt Highway in 1939. The Jesse James home stayed in place at the Belt Highway location until it was moved again in 1977 where it remains at 12th and Mitchell streets across from the historic Patee House. The house stands on a hill only two blocks from its original location.

Old St. Joe was a post card town but in spite of its captive spell, I travelled West after my Army discharge. Like many native sons and daughters, I re-visit the scenes of my growing up days. A pilgrimage every few years to the James' house and the old Patee House Museum where the Pony Express began is always on my itinerary. The old black, smoky-looking house has been restored, the hole in the wall rebuilt and layered with a floral patterned period style wall paper.

A visitor is free to wander about the house, adorned with nostalgic charm and furnishing,s to imagine the day April 3, 1882, the day Robert Ford gunned down the outlaw Jesse James. The rooms contain a collection of artifacts owned by Jesse James and his family. The exterior is painted colonial white with green shutters much like the time when Jesse James was shot. Oh, yes the bullet hole is still there in that fateful wall --

having been made much smaller to match the actual size of the glancing bullet But that gaping hole, covered with a clear frame to protect it from souvenir hunters, stares right through you.

And the picture, no longer crooked, says "God Bless Our Home."

Jesse James Home in St. Joseph

"Don't throw stones at your neighbors, if your own windows are glass."

- Poor Richard's Almanack, 1736

Banjo Coyote

One summer night
Camping by a stream
Under a whispering pine
I dreamed a whiling little dream.

A coyote strummed my banjo
He yipped at the moon above
Then sang a lonesome lullaby
Of a melancholy love

I laid there on my sleeping bag
Could not believe my ears
His song of love to the moon above
Was bringing me to tears

Thinking I must be dreaming
I flung the tent flap open
And what to my surprise
The camp was full of critters
I saw the starlight in their eyes.

"Coyote Plays the Banjo"

Art by Johnny Schultz, server at Southwest Diner

Raccoons and owls
furry critters of every kind
even the bear and deer
gave me no never mind.

They seemed all in a trance
As the coyote strummed the banjo
They began to dance

Not as sad as before
The coyote was
not lonely anymore

So we all came together
And danced the Diddley Bo
All around the camp fire
To the song of the coyote
Strumming my old banjo.
S.L.N.

SOUTHWEST
DINER

6803 Southwest Avenue• St. Louis, MO 63143
314-260-7244

SOUTHWEST DINER

I'll meet you at the Southwest Diner
in the morning
Nothin could be finer than to meet you at the Diner
in the morning
It will be your favorite spot
They pour the coffee fresh and hot
For Taos hunters wanting flavor
fiery eggs are yours to savor
the servers are the best in town
there's not a hipper place around
I'll meet you at the Diner in the morning!
S.L.N.

THE GREAT RIVER STATE

Missouri is all about rivers. It's named for the longest contiguous river in North America at about 3770 miles from the time a raindrop hits the Jefferson River until it flows into the Gulf of Mexico. The original name of the stream, Pekitanoui, means "river of the big canoes" although it has been known as the Big Muddy or Smoke-Colored River even before Europeans arrived.

The state is partly bordered on five sides by rivers: the Mississippi, the Des Moines, the St. Francois, the White, and the Missouri. We have just at 110,000 miles of flowing water, 118 of which are major enough to be considered rivers or major creeks. The actual number of streams is constantly changing, depending upon rainfall. During the 20th century most of the major streams were dammed to provide reservoirs for water, recreation and power generation, starting with the White River in 1913, forming Lake Taneycomo. Damming rivers fell out of favor in the 1970s, with the vote against the Meramec Dam, already under construction, in 1978.

In addition to traditional uses of rivers for fishing, swimming, transportation, sewage and motorized recreation. Missouri is known for its well-developed "float" industry; human powered river trips on often spring fed-streams of all sizes.

We are indeed, the "Great" River State!

SHOW ME THE RIVER TONIGHT

On the banks of the Osage River with friends around the campfire - the moonrise and star-light shining on the dark water —the memory of campfire songs and swimming in the night river still haunts my reverie.

Oh show me the river tonight,
show me the river tonight
Come all you sons and daughters
let's dance upon the waters
And show me the river tonight.

Sing down the river tonight,
Oh sing down the river tonight
Come play your guitar

‘neath the Ozark mountain stars
And sing down the river tonight.

Let’s dance by the river tonight,
let’s dance by the river tonight
Bring your banjo bring your fiddle
Let your river bottom wiggle
And dance by the river tonight

Hear the drums down the river tonight,
beat your drum by the river tonight
Let the sound reverberate
‘round this Great River State
Hear the drums down the river tonight.

Oh show me the river tonight,
show me the river tonight
come all you sons and daughters
let’s swim in the starlight waters
and show me the river tonight!
S.L.N.

Raccoon in the Ozarks

The raccoon comes down
to the water to drink. Moonlight slides
on the coal black water.

With one paw, then the other,
It reaches out, tentatively as a girl
to touch the moon face grinning
as the night fish jump.

The moon shakes as water slaps
the far rock wall. Black-green shards slip
against coon whiskers
as he turns over rock by rock

until one becomes a crawfish,
pale belly shining
in the coon moon light.
J.S.

Missouri River Suite

I.

In yellow November light
ice floats south on the Missouri
curdled cream floating on coffee--
steaming in the sun.

The long-shadowed landscape
alternates twixt blue and gray
butternut and brown--
what's not been tilled, tis been pushed around
by Ne-su-ja –great smoky water
a river whose soul's been dammed or drowned
neither wild nor free
a cougar on a choke-chain
a stallion harnessed to the plow.

II.

Campfire smoke rises
and the smell of chicory coffee.
So early, the river lies hidden
rolled in its foggy blankets.
Pans clatter to the gravel.

A fire crackles. Curses on the air
and a yelping dog flutters a flock of teal.
Breakfast voices murmur--
the water speaks back, the water slaps the shore.

When morning's curtain rises
the boat's long gone--
the only visitor remaining a turkey vulture
strutting kinglike, supping on fish heads and
rabbit's feet
scattered near the still smoldering coals.

III.
Many in vain have fenced this river.
Levees and wing dikes, dredgers and channelizers
all manner of methods to make the crooked way straight
Still, it lashes like a trick rope come spring,
an angry swollen snake forced to swallow
the snowmelt of half a continent. Bluff to bluff,
self-carved rock its only restraint, the bridges heave,
shiver as the pulse passes through. The river watches
as the humans, its alleged masters, flee for the breaks
when the wall of muddy water comes down.

IV.

Bull boats, canoes, keelboats, steamboats, dredges,
rowboats, fishboats, towboats and barges,
speedboats, pontoons, the occasional, half-mad
swimmer. In the beginning was the river.

V.

Bluecat prowls its watery murk
drifts like a submarine come dark.
When the whippoorwill trills
Bluecat rooms the chutes and pools.

Bluecat's seen it all--
Coffins in the spring, trysts in the fall.
Bluecat felt the water grow hot
when the boiler exploded, fireball thrown high
rode out the quake, met eye to eye
with the chained prisoner doomed to die.
Saw the dip of the paddle, scabbed blankets overboard
floating hemp bales stained with blood
clung in its bank hollow against the flood.
Seen the bare feet of the children of the Lord
come to be baptized at the ford–that's the most fun—
Bluecat gets to play Leviathan.

VI.

No corn grows on the Missouri Point.
Farmland gone wetland
Too thin to walk on, too wet to plow
It's the catfish year all the time, now.
Out Red Schoolhouse Rood
John's place used to yield 150 bushels
two-thirds of the time, with no fertilizer,
levee fields now tangle willow, sycamore and scrub.
No one goes there. What wasn't taken in '93
produces spring rabbits and eagles in the winter.
The house Rose cleaned year ofter year
stands hollow-eyed, stepless and empty
the porch gone by collision with a chicken coop.
Developers lust for that flat acreage
beyond the trestle, over by the slough
just can't wait to site an industrial park
under twenty feet of water.

Each spring, the people of West Alton prayed
that their town be spared--
Or if that not be His Will
That He first send the gentle Mississippi,

then send the Missouri straight to hell.

VII.

Blackjack, baccarat, slot machines and sin
boats in moats, boats afloat, craps and the lust to win!
Bright lights, jingle nights, women and whiskey
Green felt, gilded guilt, let the dice roll frisky--
Ghosts of broke gamblers past float by
From K.C. to Little Dixie.

VIII.

Twin rails tethered to the Missouri bluff
Connect the gateway to the jumping-off.
St. Louis to Westport Landing, rails and river
Past the cornfields, the wispy winter wheat.

Along the way
Houses stand like sentinels on earth pedestals
A finger in the face of the river, the former's dare
Playing out in towns like Defiance--
One hundred years of wrestling a living here
hung on the sign at the century farm.

IX.

They've paved over Gumbo Flats.
Bright boys with more money than sense
Brought dozers and steel, concrete and architects
Bought out the farmers, penned up the river
with a 500 year levee, promises and paper.

Might as well hung those hundred dollar bills
clothespinned in the sycamores along the river.
Might as well tried to fill a bucket with a strainer.
The Valley looks bright with red tail lights,
barriers on the bridges so the commuters cannot see
the brown giant slumbering beside them.
Out of sight, out of mind. Human superiority
rules like a drunken king, making money with glee
and spending it like a wenching sailor.
And then it rains.

X.

Buckskin's the rage this year, and small print calico.
Everyone's a mountain man, anxious
to conquer the river in the wrong direction.
The Missouri itself appears indifferent.

Water-striders come and go,
history just a story people tell to please themselves,
channel marker between shifting sandbars,
two hundred years a gnat's eyelash
in the inexorable flow.
J.S.

Revelation at Big Muddy

Lines Composed on the Heights Overlooking

Big Muddy National Fish & Wildlife Refuge

One day exploring the Village of Arrow Rock, I sauntered up the hill just above George Caleb Bingham's house and walked further, overlooking the grand vista of Big Muddy.

I could not see the wide Missouri through the impenetrable growth of green tanglewood and floodplain vegetation. The Big Muddy is being restored, and slowly becoming again what once was, the vast floodplain forest of giant trees, marshes and wet prairie lands I walked closer into the aura of the wilderness scene before me and as I entered into that wild space the sound and embrace of all nature engulfed my senses.

The farther I stepped into that green-hearted place the more voluminous the sound. It was a singing wilderness of bird life, thousands of insects: rhythmic buzzing cicadas, crickets chirping, flying and buzzing macro invertebrates; even the trees seemed to be talking, sighing in the summer breeze, catfish moaning in the river, the murmurings of all wildlife breathing, exhaling, living and dying....

Enthralled and enlightened by this universal choir of creation, this symphony of singing wilderness, I was reminded once again the language of the Great Spirit is all around us. We only need listen to the music.

S.L.N.

Arrow Rock Banjo Song

In the River Hills where the Big Muddy flows
where living history is alive and well
and the village charm will cast its spell

come on up, come on down,
come on down
to Arrow Rock Town

Hear the Banjo on the porch
Hear the Banjo in the street
Hear that old time Banjo sound
comin down in Arrow Rock town

Where the Santa Fe Trail took travelers west
And the Houston Tavern is still the best
Hallelujah! Hear that Banjo ringing
Somewhere there's gospel singing

Hear the Banjo on the porch
Hear the Banjo in the street
Hear that happy Banjo sound
Comin down in Arrow Rock town.
S.L.N.

The Oracle of Alley Spring

She dwells beside the shining river
Alone but not alone

She has built herself a spirit house
Stone by stone by stone

How old is the universe
And how did we begin

Was it just a singularity
Or a time that never ends?

The mysteries of the universe
Are locked in the rocks of time

She reads the rocks like a book
Like the earth in ancient rhyme

Like a geode holding secrets
From the drifting sands of time

If you wish to find her
You might find her walking there

Beside the shining waters
Under her aura of silver hair

You will hear her wisdom singing
Like flowing water from the spring:

Shannondale oh Shannondale
Your realm is in her dream
Your emerald forest and diamond waters
And the caves of Alley Spring.

S.L.N.

The Oracle Speaks Back

One magic Ozark morning
We rode the hills, slid southward
On snakeback 19, ended up
Walking the trail around Alley Spring.

The sun not yet over the mountains
The spring spilled over in half-light
First fallen leaves circled the blue eye
Damp lashes blinking on the old stone face.

What we spoke of broke the silence
Light talk to lift the curtain between us
The purpose that brought us here—
A blessed space for the oracle's speech.

Water jostled the rocks as he read,
Liquid music uniting earth and air
No tourist disturbed the private service
Only insects to witness the embrace.

We took time to climb the rocky trail out
We took the long way to the bridge
Songs sustained the spring cast spell
Paw paws on picnic table as sacrament.
J.S.

The largest measured spring discharge In Missouri was at Alley Spring, on April 22, 1974, of 1,776,000,000 gallons in a day or 2750 cfs, under very unusal hydrologic conditions.

Alley Spring Water Breath

Early morning.
The mist capped spring
Resembles blue jello beneath frothy white meringue.
Lavender shadows
Hold court beneath the trees.

It's nine o'clock.
The sun's not made it
Over the bluff.
Mist moves like cotton wadding,
Shifts downstream.

By ten, the day's grown steaming yellow-green.

As shafts of sun finger through bluff top cedars,
The mist stirs, then sun-struck, vanishes.
More cold rises and mist reforms.
For a handful of minutes,
The air plays touch and go--

With swirling visible breath
Spirit moves across the water.
J.S.

Winter Gigging on the Current

It was 15 degrees at nine at night on December 1. We bumped down the gravel road where it snakes off the end of V Highway down to Current River. I was bundled in five layers, and a sock hat, looking like an immobile kid in a snowsuit. I hoped my old hiking boots had been sprayed with enough silicone to render them waterproof. Luckily, no one could see the brand-new pink Wal-Mart wool socks.

We crunched loose rock, the front of the van pointed straight at a crowd of people in thermal coveralls and sock hats, about 15 feet below on the gravel bar. We could hear the sputtering hum of generators sparking gasoline into daylight. Fish fumes and smoke rose from a homemade cooker and nearby fire.

The driver turned left, then halted. "We can't get down there," he said. "There's a puddle all the way across the road." And proceeded to back up the narrow track towards the lights.

"I'm sure they are our people," I said, "and they got down there somehow."

Thoroughly unconvinced, he made a second attempt. "I'm not responsible if we get stuck," he said. And what happens then?"

We call a guy with a tractor or a pickup and a chain," I said. "Probably the people we're meeting have one."

When the crop of flatlanders signed up for this adventure, the night temperatures were supposed to be in the forties. Ozarks like nothing better than to play tricks on furriners.

I had barely walked into the circle of fire and halogen light, when was startled to hear "Jo, you're in my boat." An older gentleman of some modest acquaintance had laid claim, knowing full well I was the perfect captive audience for his stories.

A mess of fish heads and guts lay on the rocks, insuring there would be fish fry whether we rank amateurs caught anything or not. The boat lights blinded me as I steadied my self on the gigging rail to step up. "You stay up there, and grab that shortest gig," came the command. We took on two more passengers. The man at the helm slowly scraped the aluminum boat backwards into deeper water.

Gig boats with jets can run in mere watery inches; they often have to on Current River. I have no idea how many tens of thousands of candlepower the boat's noisy generator squeezed into the beams starboard and port. As we motored upstream, looking for fish below, my friend JC gave a running commentary of the development of gigging lights from pine knots to turpentine torches, carbide lights, coal oil, kerosene and gasoline lanterns, incandescent bulbs, spotlights, halogen lights and now extra bright LEDs which sipped gasoline like a maiden aunt at a tea party, and could run all night on four gallons of fuel.

Orion and his sparkle companions led the way on the blue velvet sky. The lights turned the dark river into liquid Coke bottle green glass flowing with motor enhanced waves. And at the bottom of that glass were fish. Misty fog skimmed the riffles like fluffy grey meringue, headed for Arkansas.

Only suckers or other rough fish can be taken by gig — a 10 to 20 foot handled, four-tined pitchfork that is used to stab them as they swim. This is a deceptively difficult task— fish are quick and not where you think they are, since both fish and pole are bent like a straw underwater.

JC talked about his son, now a highway patrolman, who started with a short gig when he was barely tall enough to top the gig rail— a three-foot tall boy with a six-foot gig.

Gigging is mostly a male sport. Later, the women standing around the fire in their Carhartt's and muck boots said they'd all done it too, but most had retreated to help cook after they married. I suppose taking your girlfriend gigging, with the secret hope she would fall in, and you'd have to get her out of her wet things before she froze to death had a certain attraction to youngsters, even in the strait-laced Ozarks.

The chill cuts on your cheeks, running the river at night. You must keep your balance upright while moving on the water, (sort of like walking on a train) while straining to see if riverbed patterns in front of the john move, or rocks are just playing tricks at riffles. Memorizing all JC's stories soon proved impossible.

In a couple rounds up and down, I only saw six fish (three off limits due to species). I tired. I'd made a couple stabs and hit nothing but rocks. The boat moves forward and the fish moves sideways. Plus, as I soon learned, if the boat runs a little fast, and the gig hits too hard on the bottom, you run the risk of having it twisted from your hands, and thrust under the boat. Not good.

JC said, "You need to come back in September. By now only the smart fish are left. You need to start early in the season if you want to learn how catch something, starting with the stupid fish." He had no idea the opening day of the season is implanted in my brain, because it happens to be my birthday

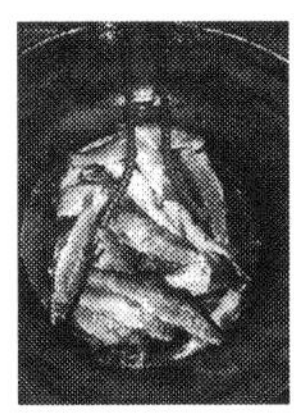

The locals, had run that stretch earlier that evening, leaving only the smartest of the smart fish for us. Their successful filets were frying for our return. One of our crew did successfully stab a yellow sucker, but the fish wriggled off the tines. Just like you track a wounded deer, we must have circled seven or eight times to retrieve that fish. Why hadn't anyone brought a net?

We landed and I splashed getting out. After photos for the fellow who caught the sucker, it was over to the fire and food, where I thought about the fish-gut party raccoons and otters would have later that night.

J.S.

(Gigging photos courtesy of Clay McNail and Thomas Counts)

Misty Waters

(for James Swiney Rayfield)

I"ve been down in those old Missouri hills
full of folks and old abandoned stills
I've seen the waters rush down the hollers there
and grown up with the trees in the clean fresh air.

I've waded in a spring branch, flowing with liquid ice
and sat around a campfire when that fire felt awful
nice,
I've looked at the stars from a gravel bar and
watched a doodlebug churn--
there are secrets there that no one'll ever learn.
Misty waters risin' and misty waters flow--
The Current River goes where it has to go.
I've seen an Ozark sunrise begin the day
an orange morning chasing away the gray--
I've listened to a blue jay squawk, his temper riled--
one of the things that makes the wild a bit more wild.
I've brewed myself some tonic, a cup of sassafras tea
and ate my share of cherries, wild cherries from the
tree.
I met some pine knot people whom I'd like to call my
friends--

but then I had to go back home again.

Misty waters risin' and misty waters flow

The Current River goes where it has to go.

J.S.

Airphoto Tufa Creek

From twenty thousand feet
the hills resemble an old man's hands
skin fitting loosely over the bones
a shawl of soil draped over stones
rivers meandering like convex veins.
At this distance
the creek does not show its face
beauty draws a blank
at thirty meter resolution
The horse trails mere spider lines
written on the weeds.
No wonder the map
calls this drainage intermittent:
the flash of water hidden beneath the trees
no hint of crystal calcite ridges
wrinkling downstream.

J.S.

The Tsalagi Syllabary

Of the 300 or more American Indian groups, the Tsalagi, or Cherokee, are one of the most well-known, perhaps because their efforts to adapt to European customs came to naught in the most tragic way, with their forced removal from the TN-GA-NC area to dry, barren OK. Their written language confounds most Americans, since it is not an alphabet, but a syllabary: a symbols stands for a pronounced syllable, jnot a letter. Not all English sounds occur in Tsalagi or vice versa, making transliteration very difficult. Sequoyah, aka George Gist, devised the "talking leaves" system without formal language education. It was approved for official use in 1825 or 1826.

Ꭰ a	Ꭱ e	Ꭲ i	Ꭳ o	Ꭴ u	Ꭵ v
Ꭶ ga Ꭷ ka	Ꭸ ge	Ꭹ gi	Ꭺ go	Ꭻ gu	Ꭼ gv
Ꭽ ha	Ꭾ he	Ꭿ hi	Ꮀ ho	Ꮁ hu	Ꮂ hv
Ꮃ la	Ꮄ le	Ꮅ li	Ꮆ lo	Ꮇ lu	Ꮈ lv
Ꮉ ma	Ꮊ me	Ꮋ mi	Ꮌ mo	Ꮍ mu	
Ꮎ na Ꮏ hna Ꮐ nah	Ꮑ ne	Ꮒ ni	Ꮓ no	Ꮔ nu	Ꮕ nv
Ꮖ qua	Ꮗ que	Ꮘ qui	Ꮙ quo	Ꮚ quu	Ꮛ quv
Ꮜ sa Ꮝ s	Ꮞ se	Ꮟ si	Ꮠ so	Ꮡ su	Ꮢ sv
Ꮣ da Ꮤ ta	Ꮥ de Ꮦ te	Ꮧ di Ꮨ ti	Ꮩ do	Ꮪ du	Ꮫ dv
Ꮬ dla Ꮭ tla	Ꮮ tle	Ꮯ tli	Ꮰ tlo	Ꮱ tlu	Ꮲ tlv
Ꮳ tsa	Ꮴ tse	Ꮵ tsi	Ꮶ tso	Ꮷ tsu	Ꮸ tsv
Ꮹ wa	Ꮺ we	Ꮻ wi	Ꮼ wo	Ꮽ wu	Ꮾ wv
Ꮿ ya	Ᏸ ye	Ᏹ yi	Ᏺ yo	Ᏻ yu	Ᏼ yv

ᏣᎳᎩ *OR* ᏣᎳᎩᎯ

Cherokee Farmer

The young Cherokee farmer Francis Gore Livingston and his wife Caroline were driven off their farm in Northwest Missouri by Confederate raiders in the fall of 1863—The year of Jubilee. They escaped north into Iowa where Livingston enlisted in the 36th Iowa Infantry on a cold December day.

We sing of his memory and service:

He's a soldier dressed in Blue;

He wakes up in the morning dew,

Marching down to Arkansas

to free the slaves one and all.

Caroline, Oh Caroline!

I'll come back to you in Summer time.

Downstream by steamer then to the Yazoo Pass, the 36th Iowa joined up with other units fighting skirmishes all the way.

He's a soldier dressed in Blue;

He wakes up in the morning dew,

Marching down to Arkansas

To free the slaves one and all

He dreams of his farm and Caroline,

Hopes to return in Summer time.

He sees first blood in the wetland fields and river mud. And Lincoln's Army marched their way on the other side of winter through the swamps and tanglewood all the way down into Arkansas.

He's a soldier dressed in Blue;

He wakes up in the morning dew,

Marching into Arkansas

To free the slaves one and all.

Caroline, Oh Caroline!

I'll come back to you in the Summer time.

His 9-pound Springfield musket is heavy, but he knows to have it ready— always ready against an ambush day or night.

The men are hungry, half-starved and the voracious mosquitos are bloodthirsty, but the men know their cause is just and they fight on. Then came the bloodiest battles yet to be fought: fought with cavalry, artillery, infantry and hand to hand—the battles of Devall's Bluff and Poison

Spring. Then Livingston was assigned to escort the First Kansas Colored and a wagon train loaded with corn. They were attacked by Southern cavalry under orders to "give no quarter" and take no prisoners: "colored soldiers" to be massacred one and all. Livingston and others make it to a row of cabins where they run out of ammunition. They were threatened with burning alive unless they surrendered. The 36th Iowa Infantry died that day on April 25th, 1864.

He's a soldier dressed in Blue;

he wakes up in the morning dew,

Marching down to Arkansas

To free the slaves one and all.

Caroline, Oh Caroline!

I'll be back in the Summer time.

Livingston and a few others were captured and forced to walk 250 miles to the infamous prisoner of war camp "Hell Hole" in Tyler, Texas.

When Juneteenth came and Texas fell, Camp Tyler was liberated and Livingston set free. The Civil War had ended. Livingston found his way back home to his farm in Northwest Missouri.

He's a soldier dressed in Blue,

He wakes up in the morning dew,

We marched down to Arkansas

To free the slaves one and all.

When the bloom is on the vine

In the greenfield day of summertime,

I'll walk back to you, Oh Caroline,

walking through your garden gate

To leave behind that world of woe, that world of hate---

No one really knows the suffering of soldiers. Only those soldiers who have made the sacrifice really know. It is an abstract concept to most of us who sit on the sidelines of history. The wrath of war is beyond our reckoning. This is dedicated to their service and their unsung courage and perseverance.

I am told that Great-Great Grandfather was never quite the same,having suffered untold deprivation and hardship, yet he and Caroline raised a family and at the time of his death in 1896 he had livestock a plenty and a barn filled with corn and oats and a two dollar a month war pension.

S.L.N.

Nunna dual Tsuny

"The Trail Where They Cried"

ᏅᏛᏗᏕᏅᏅ ᏧᏢᏃ ᏴᎾ ᎠᏠᏨᏍᏛᏗ

1830-1839

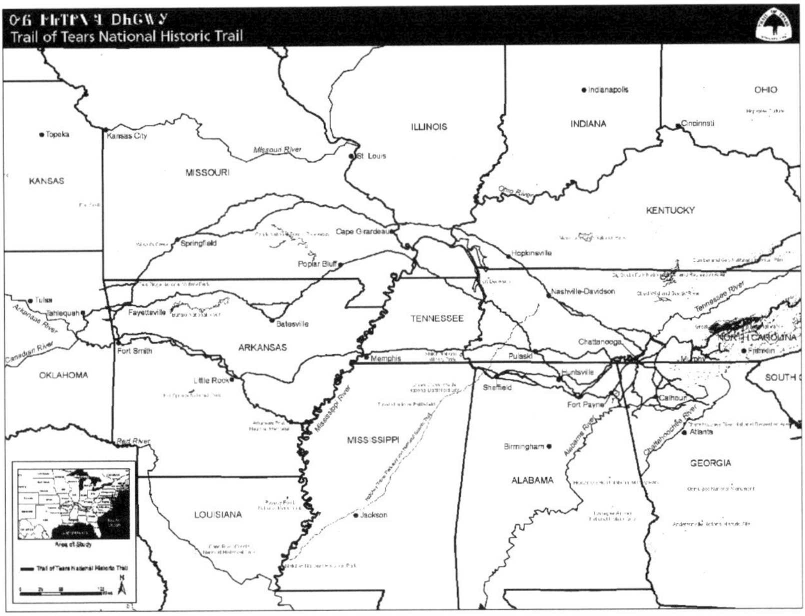

FLYING LIZARD LANGUAGES

Flying Lizard Languages LLC

825-C Merrimon Avenue #325

Asheville NC 28804

info@flyinglizardlanguages.com

A Pilgrimage to Trail of Tears State Park

By Steve Nagle, while Missouri Parks Association President. Adapted from a column published in August 2014.

OSIYO! (Cherokee for greetings!)

In March 2014, Principal Chief of the Cherokee Nation Bill John Baker said: "It was 175 years ago that the final group of our Cherokee ancestors arrived in Tahlequah, Oklahoma after forced removal on the Trail of Tears."

To memorialize the anniversary, several national events were held between then and Labor Day weekend. A proclamation was signed proclaiming the day "Cherokee Nation Remembrance Day."

What happened in 1838-39 is one of several reasons to visit Trail of Tears State Park. Having Cherokee ancestors, the visit for me was a pilgrimage of sorts, shamefully past due.

During that winter, rain, snow and freezing conditions along the northern removal route through Tennessee, Kentucky, Illinois and Missouri, trapped several thousand Cherokee men, women, children and elders on both sides of the ice-choked Mississippi river. Over 4,000 Cherokee lost their lives along this perilous path.

Ice Similar to 1838 at MoccasinSprings

The park was acquired in 1957 to commemorate the removal and the Cherokee people who died on the Trail of Tears. This park preserves the site of the northern Mississippi River crossing at Moccasin Springs, a mile of the removal route, and the Bushyhead Memorial. Nine of the 13 Cherokee groups crossed the Mississippi here.

We travelled to the park on an August Saturday to attend the annual public information meeting. Now encompassing 3,415 acres in Cape Girardeau County, Trail of Tears State Park is a true gem in the emerald necklace that makes up our state park system.

We explored the park and sampled the trails at our leisure, quite unlike the forced march of my Cherokee forebears: the nine-mile Peewah trail, three-mile Sheppard Point trail, two-mile Lake trail, and an easy half-mile nature trail.

The park is laced with very steep and rugged drainages. The river hills and bluffs make for outstanding vistas along the river. We visited Lake Boutin, the campground, and the visitor's center. Interpretive Resource Coordinator Steve Schell says the native woodlands in the park now appear much as they did to the passing Cherokee.

The last major park addition is the visitor center, built in 1988. It provides an array of cultural information, and is the location of interpretive exhibits and programs. Visitors learn that by the 1830s the Cherokee were literate, with their own written language and self-governing within a system similar to the U.S. Constitution. Most had adopted European style log cabins, personal dress and farming methods in addition to their traditional hunting activities. Many were Christians. This did not prevent federal and state officials from coveting and taking their land by fits and starts, and then entirely by forced removal after the questionable New Echota Treaty of 1835.

According to Park Manager Denise Dowling, this is the only such center along the entire northern removal route between the start in Cherokee, North Carolina, and the end at Tahlequah, Oklahoma. The park also contains Woodland Period archaeology sites listed on the Natural Register of Historic Places.

On a warm August day I hiked through the woods down to the area of the historic river crossing and pondered the scene. It must have taken many miracles and a collectively dauntless spirit to survive the long eastern part of the trail only to face the winter river crossing, enduring unimaginable hardships and an icy river crossing with scant blankets, worn clothing, and many barefoot, being prodded against their will to an unknown destination.

Today the Cherokee Nation lives and thrives again, and Missouri's Trail of Tears State Park preserves an important part of this enduring story.

To learn more about the park and the history of the Trail of Tears go to: http://mostateparks.com/park/trail-tears-state-park.

Ꮪ ᏘᏍ

The Trail Where the People Cried

The river froze that last December:
We got neither boats nor horses across.
Those who had gone earlier, willingly, resigned to fate
Had it better, but even better was not without crying:
In summer we died of malaria, cholera, dysentery;
In winter of exposure and starvation. Once across
We could not move. Ice stifled our going west
And so we starved on the far shore, or froze to death
Under stiff blankets as cold as the sheets
in which we wrapped our dead and dying.

It was not our wish to leave. Did we not, as a people,
Live in houses, farm and ranch, wear white man's clothes
and even took up his religion, intermarrying freely? We
wished what anyone wished: to work and laugh and
raise our children, to feed ourselves, to sing and dance,
to spend our days in the smoky hills of home,
drink our sweet water and trade as we had forever?

But gold and greed drove evil two-hearted men.
They preached justice on Sunday and stole
from us the other six. We finally believed

Red-Hair William Clark, agent to the Osage:
That the people of this land could not hope to live
Amongst Americans from Europe, more savage than
the Tsalagi have ever been. We agreed to go.

But no one told us of blood on the snow
The whips with which we would be driven,
The whimpered cries of dying wives and children
The sting of cold mud on frostbitten feet,
nor the harshness of blindered soldiers,
the constant digging of shallow graves
On the journey to Talequah, Oklahoma.
J.S.

Nancy Bushyhead Grave, Trail of Tears State Park

Panorama

The scenes scroll five feet high
— huge hand-turned paintings
From Lake Itaska to the Atchafalaya,
traveling slide shows
Two bits a view. The men who haul these
things, tell the story
From ancient rocks through
modern allegory, a panorama
of Indians and slaves, frontiersmen,
boatmen, the voyageurs
Up and down the Mississippi.

We'll scroll past the wharf ladies
in red dresses, grimy stevedores hauling rope;
perhaps we'll pause
in the well-lit drawing rooms aboard ship,
well-dressed card sharks
masking their deals; engine room men
facing death and disaster
around every bend. Have you seen
moonlight on these waters,
The brick streets and iron wheeled wagons
waiting, the dirt roads
hobo fires in the grapevine thickets, the points
of churches far inland,
hay stacks and cotton bales to be loaded at
morning; pewter and cloth,
preachers and teachers, books and china, and
all manner of detail?
Showboats and keel boats, box boats and rafts
bound for New Orleans-
Have you seen the greed and the speed and the
cobblestone daughters
Heard he story of the wild Mississippi,
300 feet long by 5 foot high?

J.S.

Composition in Black and Red: South St. Louis

Morning

The city squats stolidly brick and stone
built in barracks rows of family flats
fired clay streets and baked backyard dirt
where old men raise tomatoes and roses.

The cast iron fences march like daggers
barbed wire remnants the guard the lawns
white bleached stoops sit prim above them
worn by the shuffling of black-broganed feet.

Midday

Behind the brick front lies the fatherland
a disciplined chamber of German efficiency
in cool rooms of Victorian furniture
children grow on coal and the switch.

Here women stab needles in cloth and people
and rack each other until quilt-frame taut
hidden by the dark of church basement cold
they snip their scissors and call it sodality.

Night

The newsboys rumble iron wheels on brick
far away a fire truck screams in the dark
beer clouds float from the brewery to home
streetlights cast shadows on the cobblestone wharf.

The river sweeps along beside the city
towboats and barges churning brown water
Boat horns bellow like dying behemoths
Diesel engines shake the limestone bluffs.
J.S.

Jefferson Barracks From the River - St. Louis

1522 on Kirkwood Hill

Early summer. Walking to class.
Over the hills comes the plaintive wail
of the last dinosaur still breathing—
the iron behemoth struggles up the grade,
pulls the climb at Kirkwood Hill.

The throaty roar stops me still.
No one else notices much
as the damp call circles the valley
the cast metal phoenix come alive
fire in its belly breathing smoke.
Like a chimera, I never see it.

Past the buildings, beyond the trees
no less impressive for that--
the old engine spewing ciders and steam
casting a grace nearly forgotten
heaving boiler pushing the pistons still.
J.S.

The Science of Eclipses

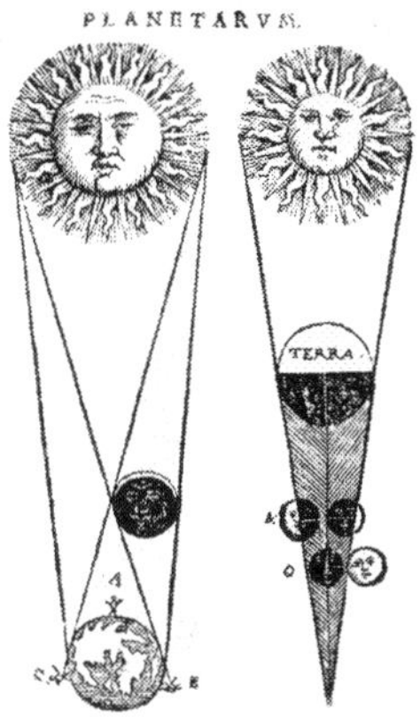

An Eclipse is a very simple alignment of the sun and earth which occur with predictable frequency. During a total eclipse, the full moon obscures the disk of the sun during daylight, creating darkeness for several minutes. Depending on the position of the sun and the observer, partial eclipses, which look like a black bite out of the sun, are possible.

On August 21, 2017, millions of Americans paused to watch the stellar show over 3 hours from Oregon to South Carolina. An annular eclipse will occur on October 14, 2023 from Oregon to Texas, and on April 8, 2024, another total eclipse will pass over the southern and midwestern United States.

> Fourteen days before or after a solar eclipse a lunar eclipse will happen, an occurence noted even by early man. J.S.

Corona during eclipse on Route 66 by Jo Schaper

The Day the Sun Went Away

The unnatural chill rises: cool breeze lofts
the hair on my arms. The change comes slowly,
Cirrus clouds scud at 20,000 feet;
sun drops evaporate one by one.

Around me, tourists in lawn chairs
lean back like cruisers on the foredeck
catching a tan. "Mother said," said one,
"You should never stare into the eye of the sun."

Except today, said the big black squirrel,
Except today, croaked the giant frog.
Bring your weapons, ready your drums,
We need everyone helping to drive away
The demon devouring the disk of the sun.

Twilight comes early. Ice breezes stir the cirrus
into transparency. Under the tent
explanation fades in favor of experiment;
A metal colander strains rays into crescents
thence into multi-pointed stars. The line to watch
the eaten sun ebbs and flows at the telescope.

The moon shadow climbs the western sky,
as it pulls the covers up. The brightest flashlight
goes dark smothered by a sky pillow. Bats whirl
into an instant dusk, a chill, silent breeze arises,
blows overhead until the cheers erupt:
the denim sky, flecked with stars, stands pierced
with a glowing, thread-edged bullet hole.
J.S.

Thelma and Doyle Johnston Tour America

Thirty years on the line makin Chryslers
bought this red trailer. We sold the house
and hit the road, V6 pickup pullin it
and we're gonna see this ol' U.S.A. Free at last,
Thel bought all 50 maps and we're gonna
drive to all of them, including Hawai'i. Ain't no one
gonna stop us, not even our kids gonna know
where we're at, free as road tramps
park at night drive by day as long as gas and money
let us. We spent thirty years watchin television
so we'll see Yellowstone of course, and L.A.
head up New York way see the penthouses
and go to Las Vegas and every neon town
along the interstate. It's gonna be
one long vacation Anaheim to Orlando
maybe stop for a baseball game somewhere
football in the fall and see them oil wells
in Texas, drive lengthwise across Kansas—
Gettysburg and Fredericksburg and Washington, D.C.
We earned it, we deserve it, and if the tires
hold out, we're going to every damned McDonalds
from sea to shining sea.

J.S.

The Returning

They rise with the river fog
pre-dawn wraiths, drenched bonnets and fedoras
faces somber with purpose.
They rise from the White, from the Osage,
the St. Francis, the Black, the Niangua--
a cortège on muleback, in wagons, on foot:
they come flaming with John Brown's fire
in the smoke of the morning--
rifles at ready, with wildcat eyes, they stalk--
they come to end it all.

With the intensity of abolitionists, they stare.
Stare at neon, at the flash of girls
whose limbs stick out like raw chicken parts
at the two-bit has-been unfunny comedians
At the constant drone of rolling, roaring tires
at come-on music drowning out the crickets,
but not flatlander unbiblical abominations.

They come.
They come like a Steuart Curry hallucination,
Benton's politicians preaching hell-fire and damnation
Gram and her shotgun, Pa and his knife.

Parading right down 76, gliding up 19,
down US 54 from the strip, over US 60--
come all the relations.

Somewhere in the morning, they meet up
with the ghosts of Bloodland,
congregate with Linn Creek's lost daughters and sons.
Theodosia and Oasis' wandering displaced
join the throngs tramping the mangled hills--
They swarm--
Like locusts, lingering only long enough
to pick the hills clean–
Glean Shoji Tabuchi's golden lounges
Crumple the turnstiles at Miner Mike's
Push down the gates of Silver Dollar City
Drain the water from Big Surf.
Ducks stop for them on Taneycomo
Chill shivers freeze tourists as they pass
moonshine runs the aisles at Moon River
a chap named Wright rings down the curtain
on the Shepherd of the Hills
Nat Kinney leads the raid
On Celebration City.
J.S.

Down Bur Oak Road

Mary Litvan-Culler

So listen,
Take the river road on a sunny day,
Cause that's where the wild things come out to play.
Where muddy flats stretch out,
And corn husks sway.
Trust me. Take the river road today.

Take time to park and watch the teals glide in,
Or spot the eagle perched atop the bluff,
And when you think you've seen enough,
Wait till dusk,
Cause that's when the wild things come out to play.

When the sun paints the river red,
Out from the rushes and the reeds,
Spring throngs of tiny peeping frogs,
That hop across the gravel road.

And glancing up the marsh a mile,
You guess there must be thousands
of these little beings,

which makes you smile.
You are not alone.

And then there comes a drone,
A jet boat flying up the river run,
Night-time seekers of Big Muddy Fun,
Their radio crackling out a good country song.

Then passing by the great Bur Oak,
You pause to say a little thanks,
For just being able to feel the cool breeze
On your face.
So trust me. Let your heart go wild and
Take the river road today.

**The poem Down Bur Oak Road was written after visiting Eagle Bluffs Conservation Area near McBaine, Missouri on a summer evening in 2007. The state champion bur oak tree (the largest bur oak tree in Missouri) is located on Bur Oak Road north of the conservation area and the town of McBaine. The great tree stands alone, surrounded by a large crop field, within the floodplain of the Missouri River.

Thunderbird - Washington State Park - JS photo

Petroglyph

When the bird flew off from the stone
the stone froze solid, the bird's bed
preserved for centuries. The white people—
they could not see: they imagined
some craftsman, pecking rock on rock
for an eternity of afternoons
some shoulder-aching meditation to
some nature god. Likewise
when the snake uncurled, sped off
into the grass after a mouse, the spiral stayed.

In those days, where one rested on the earth
transformed it; even man and maiden
in hazy morning made their marks. When
stone was dry and gritty, the passing of things
left ochre marks, powder fingerprints etched
then seared into floors and walls.

Only the few still see that doorway, low and stooped,
to the chamber where sun and moon rested
before red hands flung them skyward, the giant atlatl
slinging them into orbit, their imprints
slowly eroding under rain and ice,
that older world immanent with
the power of earth and sky--
Thrown out of the garden, we go to enter there.
J.S.

Osages - 1854   Painting by George Catlin

They Came Before Us:
Franklin County Indians and Archaeology

by Jim Duncan, St. Louis, Missouri

Franklin County's many river valleys, its location in the northeast Ozarks, with easy access to several distinct natural communities, made it a highly desirable place for ancient American Indians to live. The Ozark border and river corridors were stable ecosystems, and provided attractive food sources for ancestors of modern American Indians, for the first 15,000 or more years people were on this continent.

• In the last 80 years, numerous archaeological collections have been made in Franklin County. Every cultural period is well represented in these collections. Beginning in the early 19th century, several Pleistocene bone beds were discovered and extinct mammal bones collected, mostly by amateurs. The Missouri Archaeological Society surveys of the 1930s through 1990s, located several important Clovis sites (13,500 to roughly 12,000 years old) in the county. Clovis points have been found elsewhere in close proximity to mastodon bones.

• The late PaleoIndian Dalton culture (10,500 to 8900 years ago) is well represented in the county. Sadly, artifact collectors have destroyed many of the cave and rock shelter floors that are so important to the understanding of ancient day-to-day living. By the end of the PaleoIndian period, the climate had warmed, and the large Pleistocene mammals had become extinct.

• The long Archaic period (8900 to 2500 years ago) is well represented in Franklin County, especially the Middle and Late Archaic periods. It was then that agriculture began, probably by the work of women. The archaeological record started to show charred seeds and plant remains in fireplaces and trash pits. The villages grew during Late Archaic times, with large "earth lodge" style structures being used for winter quarters. The Late Archaic in Franklin County included large villages and numerous hamlets.

• The Woodland period (2400-1600 years ago) populations were especially drawn to the northeastern part of Franklin County. Around 1500 years ago, intensive agriculture involving plants like may grass, knot weed, chenopodium, and marsh elder, (weeds to today's farmers!), ushered in another large population increase. This in turn developed into the spectacular Western Mississippian cultural period.

• The Cahokia, or Western Mississippian people (1200 -500 years ago or 800-@1400 CE) created the largest mound groups in North America. These groups extended from the Missouri-Mississippi river junction to the Ohio-Mississippi confluence. At the height of Cahokia, Franklin County was a far-flung suburb of that great city. The county contains the only monumental pictograph that survives from Cahokia's powerful influence. This is a meter tall figure of a dancing warrior called "Morning Star" with a large rectangular shield and a war club This figure adorns Rattle Snake Bluff. Most pictographs in the county date to this period.

• The historic Nations in Franklin County (1600-1820 CE) were the Osage, who were the descendants of the Cahokian Western Mississippians, and several nations who were driven from their eastern lands during the Indian Removal period. The Osage had trading agreements with the French, but relations with the American settlers were uneven, sometimes friendly, sometimes not. After the 1808 treaty to relinquish their Missouri lands to the United States, they continued to hunt the region until statehood.

• The Cherokee, Shawnee, Miami, Delaware and others were moved into the area to serve as a buffer between the Imperial Osage by the Spanish who had become the governing power, temporarily, before being pushed further west. Shawneetown (Rogerstown), near the Chouteau Claim Access where the Bourbeuse joined the Meramec, consisted of about 40 Shawnee and Delaware families who had largely adopted European customs. The settlement was shown on area maps predating the county. As white settlement advanced, Shawneetown residents settled to the southwest in Boone Township before leaving the county entirely.

Mishebishu

Drawn in black
round otter head with a raccoon mask
deer antlers like tributaries branching
above carnivorous teeth.
They follow me
like the eyes of a trick painting
in the flicker filled light
illuminating the damp sandstone walls.

As above, so below.
I do not fathom this attraction.
Tracking ancestry from the tellers of tales
Leads to an Algonkian past.
I trespass into another's myths
and still do not know what to make of this
water-monster, spirit of underground
scribed on my cavern walls.

I bring tobacco, sweetgrass and cedar
turn off the electric, kindle aromatic fire
and far off, hear my heart beat
like the roar of distant drums.

I wait.
Wait for what I do not know.
They tell me this was a burial place
a chamber of initiation.
Red and black figures dance
on the walls where so many Europeans
scribbled their names,
heedless of the ochre values they overwrote—
defacing sand whose surface kept the pigment
for nearly a thousand years.

The spirit still lives.
--Mishebishu—
alien visitor or not, I can hear
the hissy scream caught in its rock throat

feel the baleful stare
demanding sacrifice.
J.S.

Paw Paws Reprise

It's a secret we keep
down in Missouri
In the damp forest
where the paw paws grow
a delightful fruit, too exotic
to be shared lightly. Some say
it tastes like banana, like mangoes
or papaya, all mixed up.

It's the juicy fruit essence
of Carmen Miranda's hat puréed,
to be tasted, not just looked at
in the secret green fern grottos
where the wild paw paws grow.
J.S.

About Paw Paw Poets Publishing

Paw Paw Poets Publishing is a joint venture small press between Steve L. Nagle and Jo Schaper, owner of Geo Communications Services. Both authors write poetry and prose and aim to publish both individual and joint projects about the outdoors, the Midwest and West, regional cultural and natural history, rivers, parks and other outdoor spaces. *Rendezous and other Poems of Forest Park* by Steve *was* their first publication, and the Paw Paw Almanac and Reader is their first book together.

Paw Paw Poets Publishing can be reached via http://pawpawpoetspublishing.com or https://facebook.com/pawpawpoets/ or via email at pawpawpoets@gmail.com.

Steve can be reached at stevelivingstonnagle@gmail.com and Jo at jo.a.schaper@gmail.com.